"Writing isn't about making money, getting famous, getting dates, getting laid, or making friends. In the end it's about enriching the lives of those who will read your work, and enriching your own life as well. It's about getting up, getting well, and getting over. Getting happy, okay? Getting happy."

-Stephen King

"I hate myself and I want to die."

-Kurt Cobain

--- For You ---

Please Keep Loving Me

please
keep loving me
when the thought
of losing
what we are
feels
like death's cold breath
on the backs
of our necks.

when we are
lumps in throats
and when we are
butterflies
in stomachs.

please keep loving me
when it does not come
so naturally.

when it is not easy,
when it feels
more like work
than like play.

please,
keep loving me.

please keep loving me

when,
through my blind carelessness
or
my dishonesty
I scratch open our old wounds.

when our wild animal hearts
begin to tug at their chains,
cursing everything that holds them home.

please keep loving me.

when your eye wanders
more often than it watches over me,
and when your body lusts for
new adventures,
love me.

if ever the shadow you cast
colors a darker shade
the pillows,
the blankets,
the body of another,
lying
in a place that feels more like
the scene of a terrible crime
than like a home
even then,
especially then…

please keep loving me.

and when old faults are
far behind us,
let's laugh at the day we're living
and happily go where it takes us.

let's hold the brightest of hopes
for tomorrow
and the day after that.

love me
when we make copies of ourselves
and spend decades
mixing in the best ingredients
we each have to offer.

through all of that
as challenging as it will be,
please keep loving me.

one day
those children
will move away
to search for love,
love like their parents had.

and we will make our circle small again.

in times when
our perfect harmony
is the envy
of all of our friends,
of course
you'll keep loving me

but
love me just as well
when that perfect harmony
is really nothing more
than a mirage our friends see

from their
desolate perspectives.

when I'm the boat
and you are the sea
I'll try to be a wave
or the wind
or the shore
something more a part of you
than something
to depend on you.

but we can't help what we are
and for a short time
we may refuse to flow together.

please keep loving me
while we wait for calmer weather,
the safety of low tide.

and then in those last years
when what's left of old tattoos,
fading blue blotches
are joined
by brown spots of age
marking our crinkled skin,
please keep loving me.

when the house we bought
with money we earned by
selling off
our youthful years

starts
to fall apart.

when the paint chips
and the pipes leak
when our floorboards
and our walls give way to wind
and our hallways
creak and shiver,
when the roof beings
to let in the rain...

when our love pushes up
with the same strength
as the gravity pulling everything down,
we can hold that old house together.

then
when even more years have escaped
and our sons and daughters
come home for the holidays,
they'll bring us pamphlets from rest homes
in hopes of coaxing us
from the only comfort we've ever known,
when that happens darling,
let's try to remember
they only mean the best for us.

they only mean
the best for all of us.

love me

when they've taken us away,
love me
when we're making new friends
with old souls
smiling at us across card tables
rolling around in parades of wheelchairs,
shuffling by on canes and crutches.
love me
as we wait out the twilight in buffet lines.

and when we've settled on
rusting up
and dying of natural causes,
love me as you watch me
being scooped up off the floor
by a staff of well trained strangers.

before

during

and after all of this
love me.

I will love you.

when my sight finally
begins to fail
as we're coming to the end
I hope we can still clearly see

the many reasons
we chose
to spend the only lives we had
together.

when all of this truth
comes to be,
please,
please keep loving me.

Trading Shadows

happiness

it's a conscious decision
I have to make every day.

to be "happy"
or whatever that means.

to fight that cloud above me
sky full of
dread and doom
always up above me
as if I mixed up my heavens
and my hells.

a smile
it's gotta be something I force
some days.

otherwise
happy
just seems like an impossible way to feel.

I wake up
try to wipe the dirt off the dream.

spit shine what's left of confidence,
shake my heart back to life again
and trade some of my shadows
for a little bit of sunshine.

Waiting Rooms

doctors
nurses
running around
blood tests
big scary machines
whirring and clicking and beeping.
the tubes
the screens and
the wires
the loudspeaker in the hallway
calling out codes
calling all cars
its all over for someone.

this time they wouldn't let me follow you
as they took you away.

so when the speakers call out codes
I crane my neck
to get a view down the hall
but it's all zipped up
curtains

cocoons
each with a twisted up
little worm inside.

and either that little worm is
gonna sprout wet wrinkled wings

and eventually fly off
or they scoop out
that broken little worm
and throw it away.

I closed my eyes
and rested my head against the wall
hoped for the best
I hoped for anything but
the worst.

Lost Boy In A Coffee Can

somebody's fucking
in my bedroom.

cooking food I hate
in my kitchen.

my hand prints
were in the cement
before they blew that up
and stuck a swimming pool there.

I buried a coffee can time capsule
somewhere in the yard
I filled it with trinkets and toys,
photos I tore out of magazines,
newspaper articles
and a letter I wrote
addressed to my future self.

the house I grew up in
is now somebody else's house
and they're growing up in there.

truth is
it never belonged to me
it never belonged to my family
it was just our turn
to take up that space
and when I find myself
looking at everything this way
this blink of life

seems all the more
temporary.

Youth And The Gravity Of Love

that would be *real* poetry.

the police and the ambulance would show up
and they would find my young body
squished in the road
busted up
bloody
and bloated

they'd go through my pockets
and they'd find my suicide note
crumpled up in my jeans,
scribbled and scratched in red ink:

"from now on
I won't be looking
before I cross the street
and when they print my
dead name
in the newspapers
she will know I am gone
because of her"

how silly youth in love can be.

now I can hardly recall
anything more
than the color of her hair.

Static

there are people who are born,
watch some TV
then die.

I want to live
a different life.

I want to live
a life
too big for any screen,
too loud for any speakers.

I want to live
a life that spills over the borders
and off the canvas,
a life that jumps from the page.

Dearest Tomorrow,
Please Let Me Down Easy This Time

I'm making funeral arrangements
for all of my hopes
and my dreams
and I'm just ironing out the details now
but it's shaping up to be
the party of the decade.

really,
the place to be for all eternity.

and I wish nothing more than
to show everyone a good time
while we all grieve the loss
of such promising,
hopeful little childish thoughts
of what glory might be.

Old Orchard City

an old man walked up to me
and he said
this place is all fucked up now,
he said he liked it better
how it was before.

and I told him
that I agreed.

I told him
I thought the same thing.

they've knocked down
all the old buildings
and they've gone and replaced them
with these stupid little
pastel colored stucco boxes
all stamped out
by the same cookie cutter.

they tore down
my favorite old movie theater,
I thought it was some kind of
protected landmark.

but now
right where the theater once stood
is the parking lot
for another
electronics superstore.

it's like nothing is sacred anymore.

they laid down six lanes of freeway
right through the neighborhood where I grew up,
it's all changed,
my old school is gone now too.

the old man let out a long sigh
and he shook his head,
he took his glasses off,
put his hands on his hips
and he glared at me.

I saw in his eyes
equal portions of disappointment
pity
and disbelief...

he said
"when I said I liked it better before
I meant
before those old buildings
were even built
when this valley
was nothing but orchards,
apricots
apples
almonds and walnuts.

before that old movie theater,
before that freeway,
before your old neighborhood
before your old school and
way before you.

now it's all fucked up."

It All Starts
With A Deep Breath
And A Smile

just have to remind myself
every once in a while.

this shitty place
all dark and unkind,
just dealing with it…

this tangled
rat's nest
my conscience
my guilt
the burden.

I tell myself
no matter how bad I feel
no matter how tough this life can be
I'm sure it beats rotting in the ground.

I fight a daily battle.

and when it's worse
that it has ever been before,
it takes a turn for even worse than that.
I say it to myself again,
it must beat lying in a box
rotting down there in the dirt.

I'm punching my way

out of a black burlap sack
fighting through a long string
of terrible days

must beat feeding worms
I say
must beat feeding worms,
feasting on this
rancid hunk of meat
that was my heart
my lungs
my skilled little hands,
my pretty eyes.

my old love
will poke through the surface
as a little patch of daisies
my black cloud
will push up through the dirt
as an ugly patch of weeds.

I say
I beg
I plead with myself to stay

what's my rush?
I've got forever to rot in heaven
forever to mold in the mud.

more likely there's nothing
after the shit
so
what's the point
of rushing to a red light?

say bullshit to myself when I feel

a bad streak coming on

it all starts with a deep breath and a smile.

if I take that deep breath
I can't help but feel a tiny bit better
and if I force that smile
fake that grin
no matter what
I gotta feel
a little less like the universe is collapsing
on top of me.

trouble is
sometimes
deep breaths and smiles
are really hard to come by.

so I'm asking you here,
hoping you can help me,
if maybe you can try
to keep an eye out
for someone like me
spending too much time
staring at my feet
when I'm walking,
so slowly home.

could you please?
look out for someone like me,
running low on laughs
running out of hugs
running out of love
or hope
for anything
ever getting better.

if you see me
remind me,
please,
whatever it is that hurts
it sure beats feeding worms.

let me know
somebody gives a shit.

tap me on the shoulder as I try to pass you by,
tell me to take that deep breath
tell me to fake that great big smile
and maybe if I just can't manage to,
you could lend me a smile
until I find my own.

Alice In Fuck-It-Land

he's going down that rabbit hole...

oh
I hate it when they say that.

calling it a rabbit hole
makes it sound cute.

oh no.

I'm going down the rabbit hole.

like it's some little fairy tale portal
to a magical land of
singing flowers and
smart ass cats,
caterpillars,
opium dreams.

this isn't a rabbit hole.

it's a fucking trap door
straight to hell
and when it opens,
when the floor falls out from under me
this is no fucking rabbit hole.

this is a **blackening of everything,**
it's not just a layer
of black paint
on everything.

it's the air catching fire,
it's all the pretty colors of the world
sucked out by something bigger than myself,
leaving empty grey boxes
shaped like things that were alive,
dead grass
dead leaves
dead me.

it's everything that should make me smile
just passing by,
it's the way the street starts to stink,
it's how everything in the mirror is just wrong,
the neighbor's barking dog,
it's everything I've ever done wrong
lined up to throw a punch,
glowing eyes in the bushes,
animals of guilt and weak apologies,
it's the politicians on TV
finally getting their point across,
I'm fucked
you're fucked,
everybody's fucked.

this isn't a cartoon.

this isn't a rabbit hole.

this is how I'm going to die.

Like Rats

hiding in cracks
beneath the rubble of a city at war,
they wait for the sound
of the bombs to die down
then they creep out from
the darkness of their bunkers
into the sunlight
to feed
on the flesh
of all the fallen heroes.

just a warning,
these are your friends
when you come into money.

Sometimes A Friend
Is All You Really Need

for a few strange days in the summer
I carried a pair
of little plastic eyes in my pocket.

they were those little, clear half-dome things
with the little black disc wiggling in the middle.

I don't know why I had them
but I would take them out of my pocket
cup them in my hand
and ask them questions.

maybe this is what other people do
with a
little plastic Jesus.

I think it started off as a joke,
a game I played by myself.

it eventually got so I
couldn't leave the house
without them.

a few times
after I had already left the house,
I'd realize they weren't in my pocket
and I would turn around
and go back home to get them.

I'm not even sure where they came from,

but there I was at work,
I was sitting in a meeting and I pulled my hand
out of my pocket
and there they were
mixed in with
a receipt for some tacos,
a couple balls of lint,
loose change
and them,
stuck to the tip of my finger,
two little eyes
looking right back at me.

I said hello.

they said hi.

two people in the meeting started to argue
about something
pretty passionately,
I mean they were raising their voices,
one of them stood up so fast and hard
his rolling chair shot back behind him
and crashed into the wall,
the room suddenly felt very tense,
he pointed his finger at the other guy
who was now also standing up,
people were waving their arms around,
it got loud for a minute,
but then
in my head
it quieted down...

what a bunch of assholes, right?
I said,
and the eyes on my finger,
they agreed.

then they asked me
if these people always acted this way,
I said they do
and I'm tired of it.

we were in a room full of assholes,
assholes who always
act this way
but we didn't have to listen to them
if we didn't want to.

I asked the eyes where they came from
and they said they came from my pocket,
then they asked me where I came from.

strangely
I don't think anyone had ever asked me that before,
I was born in a hospital,
I said,
I don't remember which hospital it was
but my mother said that it had been torn down
just a few years after I was born.

the eyes said it must be weird to know
that the building where I was born
has since disappeared,
again,
something I'd never really thought about before.

I asked the eyes to excuse me for a moment
and I put them away
so that I could listen to the assholes talking
just to be sure
none of them were talking
about me,
and sure enough they were doing just that!

I asked the whole room,
"are you assholes talking about me now?"

that's when all the assholes hushed,
they looked at me like I had just taken a shit on the floor.

one of the assholes cleared his throat
and smirked at me
then he shook his head.

don't know what was going on,
didn't care.

I put my hand in my pocket
and I took out the eyes again,
this time one eye was on the tip
of my middle finger
and the other
was stuck
crooked on the tip of my pointer finger.

I liked how they were
the perfect size to make heads of my fingers
just right to rest in my palm
and make a big old funny face.

they stuck to whatever
they just waited to hang out with me.

did you ever read that book
The Indian In The Cupboard?
it was about a boy who had this plastic Indian toy
and he would put it in this little cupboard
and close the door,
then when he would open the door
the little Indian would be alive!
could you believe it?
how great that would be.

assholes started standing up again
I guess it was time for the meeting to be over,
the two assholes who were yelling before
were shaking hands over the table,
other assholes were patting each other on the back.

I pasted a proud look on my face
pretended to be happy with the outcome
of our meeting
we accomplished a lot in conference room,
for sure.

I kept my left hand in my pocket
hugging my new friend,
little stowaways on the handshake parade
yes, yes,
nodding heads say things like
"fantastic!"
"impressive numbers!"
"great teamwork, everyone"
I said I really loved the direction we were headed,
and I said wow a lot.

nobody heard anything I said anyway
they never did

I don't think most of the assholes even knew
what I did there at work,
but all of the assholes were pleased
and so was I.

I took my hand out of my pocket again,
the eyes said I did a great job,
I smiled and thanked them.

maybe this whole thing started as
something I would do to give myself
a little chuckle
in the middle of a shitty day
but it all made perfect sense to me now.
felt natural.

the way a guy talks to his dog
about everything that went wrong,
got stuck in bumper to bumper traffic,
missed a deadline,
lost a huge account –
could ya believe that, Sparky?

dogs bark back,
they wag their tails and they beg.
a dog gets so excited to see you,
it'll piss on the floor
just thinking about getting your attention.

that's great for some people,
but I guess I need more than barking
and puddles of piss on my floor,
I need advice,
I need someone who'd understand
the way I feel,
someone who'd understand

what I'm saying,
not just my tone of voice.

so all the assholes left the meeting room
and walked through the maze of cubicles to their spots,
the eyes and I
decided we should leave work early.

so we snuck out through the break room
and we ran to catch the train.

we talked all the way home
about politics,
music, movies and pussy.

we laughed really hard
thinking of the fun we could have
playing pranks on the assholes at the office;
blackmailing them,
running payroll scams,
we talked about which office bitches
we would fuck if we had the chance,
if we could ever
get them alone.

this was how it should be all the time.

a real friend listens,
a real friend is loyal,
a real friend offers up some wise advice
straight from the heart.
as the train started to get more
and more crowded,

more assholes squeezed in
at each stop
and they avoided the empty seat
next to us,
they must have though we were crazy.

Abortion

my life is mine.

I can end it

I choose the time.

Thanks Be For Each Day

you grow into these back aches
and bad eyes
and you say
even though you're old now
it just feels
like life is too short.

well,
we aren't even supposed to live this long
we were not
designed
for longevity.

before your back gets sore
you're supposed to have been
eaten by an animal,
bitten by something poisonous.

before your eyes gave out
you should have had
some sort of infection in a wound
that never healed up.

you
should have fallen off a cliff
or off a snapped branch
in a fruit tree
broken bone in your back
or in your neck.

you should have been baked in the sun
or starved to death
before your legs got slow…

without all this progress
the manmade things
the medicines,
food, walls, blankets
and ideas
you probably never would have
made it to a day
when you find your first grey hair.

so when you think of saying
something like
oh, how short life is –
just try and remember
how short
it was supposed to be.

maybe think about
how lucky
you really are.

Another Rainy Day Parade, Courtesy Of Yours Truly

I've always had fun telling kids
that the business
of trying to make money
out of art,
at least what I know of this
bullshit alchemy,
is nothing but a lifelong orgy
of liars,
parodies and badly written characters
pulling dicks and
sucking blood
until there's nothing
to believe in.

it's a snake pit.

a fool's errand.

a farce.

keep your dreams to yourself,
I tell them,
that way they're safe
and they can live forever.

Post Office Box

no mail today.

walked to the box and
stuck the key in the hole,
opened the little door and I looked inside but
no mail today.

no letter to say
how important
someone thinks I am,
to say how much
what I've been doing
is helping -
doing some good.

no thanks.

no admiration,
attention
no love.

no letters from far away family.

no postcard
from her
traveling
without me.

nothing today from the government.

I'd be happy

when I open that box,
to see an envelope,
even if it's just another bill,
another notification of late payment,
threats from collection agencies,
I'd be happy when I open that box
to see a piece of paper
to prove I exist.

but no.

no mail today.

When They Close For Good

blinked.

and I'm starting to lose my optimistic,
childish determination
I'm starting to lose that drive to get something done.

blinked.

and my sense of humor is growing callous,
I'm harder and harder to tickle.

I'm starting to lose my lusting blood
it's all feeling less like a sweet indulgence
more like a sickness
or a chore, a tool to prove something
I'm not sure I believe.

I'm starting to lose my grip
on my lifelong dreams.

blinked.

and I'm starting to lose my hair,
I'm losing my nerve,
I'm losing whatever part it was in me
that let me think I could keep this up.
I'm losing my courage
I'm losing my edge
and my friends
and all the shit I thought
I might manage to hold onto forever.

Start Having Sex With A Stranger

maybe the next best thing to killing yourself
could be to change yourself
so drastically
that nobody recognizes you anymore.

fuck it all.

quit your job
quit your hobbies
quit your band
quit your love
and quit your friends
give up habits
change your phone number
move to a new town
throw a dart at a map on the wall,
stop answering to old nicknames,
stop answering to any names,
dress in bright colors
buy expensive clothes
costumes,
be someone made of nothing
but pure bullshit.

start having sex with a stranger
someone who didn't grow up in your hometown.

fuck someone who thinks
so highly of this
new scarecrow effigy made of shit.

fuck someone who thinks you're the most
interesting,
charming man.
far more independent
and original
than you could ever be.

I suggest you not make love to this person.
fuck this person really hard and good.

get a man's job
doing something tough
like roofing
plumbing
construction,
fix cars or load trucks,
cut down trees or kill animals
build skyscrapers –
don't trade stock
don't design things
or make art
don't serve food or
bake cupcakes;
none of that soft shit will make your hands
strong
and rough,
your shoulders big and broad,
baking cupcakes won't give you
the eyes of a predator.

what a woman wants
is to be fucked really hard by
a creature that's the opposite of herself.
she wants something big and hard
inside her
small and soft.

this is how you make your own life worth living again.

go back to school,
be an old fart
sitting in the back of the class
in his filthy work clothes,
muddy work boots
and big rough hands,
eyes of a predator,
teach the young girls
what it means
to get fucked for real
by a man who doesn't
apologize,
a man who makes no excuses,
puts his big fucking dick where he wants to put it,
even if she cries,
it's what god wanted to happen,
that's how he laid it out.
or, fuck god,
take a leaping lack of faith in tomorrow
fuck out that fear
holding you back for years
fuck that pussy little inner child,
fuck melting like a ball of pink wax
just because time says it's what you're supposed to do.

buy a gun
shoot a bear.

be a man.

don't let time get its filthy hands on you,

close your eyes if you're squeamish,
plug your nose,
say a prayer and jump.

jump into a new tomorrow,
not just another today you haven't slept through,
just a today
you haven't had a chance to waste.

Chores

got to a point,
so low that making my plans to die
felt as normal
as making plans to go grocery shopping,
as plain as any daily chores.

grab the keys,
get in the car,
drive to the store
fill up the cart and pay the cashier,
come home and put it all away.

grab the keys,
get in the car,
drive to the bridge
park the car and walk halfway across,
say goodbye to all the nothing.

no crying.
no scribbled notes of apology,
no tear soaked page
laying blame,
making excuses.

until then
that was the worst I've been.

that's the closest I've come.

when the plans seemed
so easy and so
dangerously logical.

Hard To Love

I miss you,
sometimes more
when you're in my arms
than when we're
separated
by a million miles.

I know it's my fault,
I've become someone
so hard to love.

The Explosions We Survive

of course we all survive
some small explosions.

from time to time we find ourselves
gingerly plucking shards of metal
from our arms and legs.

we leave these
little holes,
they end up closing on their own.

then, in their places,
grow
soft patches
of foreign new skin,
not yet ours.

with time
we may lose track of how scars happen
we may lose count
of the times we've been hurt.

of course
we all survive some
small explosions.

Tall Mistakes
Like A Forest Around Me

guilt
hangs like a weight around my neck
I carry it with me everywhere.

seeds I planted
my little lies.

acorns to oaks.

seeds to sunflowers
six feet high.

these things have a way
of getting bigger and bigger
every day.

turn my back on them a minute
and I find myself in a maze.

my doctor says

"failure is an event
not a person"

I can't help but disagree.

a piece of shit is a piece of shit.

Green Grass, Blue Sky,
Black Heart.

I have broken a few hearts
into little bits
but,
like they say,
if you want to make an omelet
you gotta break some eggs.

this one egg
many years ago
was really truly as perfect
as any egg I'd ever had
trouble was,
she wasn't right for me at the time,
to be honest I don't even know what it was
or why I just fell out of love with her,
these things happen from time to time,
maybe she was better off,
I told myself,
with someone who had a plan
a nice boy who was going to college,
she didn't need to be tethered to
someone like me
a punk sleeping in cars
and on park benches,
eating up drugs and pissing his life away -
for her own good
I had to cut her loose

so I sat her down and I told her
she was perfect,

perfect for someone else.

at the time those seemed like
the right words.

looking back it's easy to see,
there was probably a better way to say it.

but what's done is done.

my version of the old
it's-not-you-it's-me
stung a little worse
than it had to.

I actually thought
she would think it was a sweet way
to let her down easy.

I've only seen a person
cry that hard
a few times in my life
and all those other times
it was because somebody died.

some of the other eggs I broke,
I just ran away,
I'd just take off to a different city
and I'd stop answering my phone.

of course I'd end up with an epic collection
of recorded messages,
I sometimes wish I kept them all
like a twisted little best-of compilation,
blood curdling recordings,
the sound of a heart being ripped to shreds,

I captured the sounds
from a safe distance.

ring ring ring…
I've grown tired of you,
I hate your naked body and I've decided
I never want to fuck it again,
please scream your message after the beep.

I took this one,
a blonde with a big ass
much taller than me
and almost ten years older,
she really loved me
but it was time for me to move on,
I took her to a grassy hill
and I felt like an executioner.
I lifted my axe
and I chopped her head off.

she thought everything was fine,
there we were
enjoying a sunny day,
green grass,
blue sky,
black heart.

I had to follow my heart
and I had to follow my dick,
I was a young man,
and that's what young men do.

Keep Calm

I try to see
the bright side.

I try to cheer people up,
tell them
it's gonna work out
for the best.

and I really do believe
things are rarely
even half as bad as we think.

when we rush around
most of what we're killing ourselves over
just isn't so urgent
not so important.

it can wait.

stop and say that to yourself,
out loud.

it can wait.

and the things that
make us want to die
they're hardly worth a bead of sweat,
much less a drop of blood.

say that to yourself.

there's this thing
called
right now,
and I'm not very good at grabbing it
but just knowing it's there
right now
is a start.

right now
nothing's really that bad.

I Carry Mine, You Carry Yours

everyone walks around
with their own bag of shit.

the bag gets bigger every year
and more shit fills it up.

sometimes somebody comes along
they want you
to carry their bag of shit
for them.
because they just can't carry it
on their own
they just don't have the strength.

don't do it.

other people
never want to carry
their own bag of shit.

and they'll try to hang it around your neck,
so there you are
holding your own bag of shit
and you've got all these other people's bags of shit
bags of shit in each hand,
bags of shit tied to your belt,
bags of shit strapped to your back
bags of shit that's not yours
and it's
weighing you down.

you shouldn't have to carry
anyone's bag of shit
but your own.

it's hard to do
but sometimes
you just have to say no.

be empathetic
be sympathetic
above all else
try to love,

but carry your own bag of shit
and let other people
carry theirs.

Dreams Don't Come True
Just Because You Want Them To

each morning
I have to get out of bed
and put one foot in front of the other.

I have to push
and I have to pull.

things will happen
all the time
that will make me wonder
if it's worth the trouble.

if maybe I should just
give up
and settle for less
than what I've always wanted...

it's not the hard work that grates on me
and wears me down,
I don't mind working hard.

the parts that are so difficult
are the moments when I have to make those decisions –
to stop
or to keep going.

my life has been
one dream come true after another
with some tears in between.

The Nature Of Trust

you can take back words
but you can't take back touch.

it's the taste
of your blood
in the bath tub
long after you've left us.

it's the fate of lust
and the faith I've lost
this is a waste
the nature of trust.

even if she thinks she's forgiven me,
she hasn't.

even if I think
I've forgotten
for a second
the pain I've caused,
I haven't.

Different Kisses

bottom lip
bitten,
lingering after the kiss

waiting
an atom apart
for the next

the one that makes
the rest of the world go away

hot fighting tongues
wrestling in
the space
where two become one.

then years later
the kisses
are closed
and dry
and quick.

not much more than
a high five.

Fall Asleep On A Beach

I was asleep
on a beach.

and it was a gorgeous day.

the sun was shining
and the sea
was calm.

the breeze
came over me
soft and slow
all of it
something like a lullaby.

I'm Sorry I Threw A Rock At Your Head

when I was
just a little guy
throwing railroad rocks
at other kids
seemed like an alright thing to do
so long as
I was far enough away
to duck for the cover of bushes
while the rock was still in flight.

not much else to do
while you're walking home from school.

one afternoon
I picked up a large white stone
and I threw it as far as I could.

the rock made this crazy curve to the left
crescent moon
and it bounced off some kid's head.

I could hardly believe it,
what an amazing throw!

anybody else see that?

of course not.

I walked home from school
alone most days.

it wasn't until the kid
went squealing past me
running with both hands covering
a bloody fountain between the fingers
at the top of his head.

and his scream
was constant
bouncing with his steps...

ahh gahh ahh gahh ahh gahh,
oh my god oh my god.

I think I laughed as he ran by,
more out of shock and disbelief
than anything else.

it's so strange to me now
that I could ever have done
such a horrible thing.

I could never do something like that now.

I'm not that person anymore.

I didn't really feel bad about the whole thing
until the next day,
walking home
in awe of how long that trail of blood spots
drew a line along the tracks
a zig-zag of little red dots
must have been a hundred yards.

I'm not even sure
if that kid ever came back to school,
don't think I'd ever seen him before or since.

Arthritis And Box Office Gold

it's like a scene in one of those action movies
where the handsome archeologist finds himself
in some dank and dusty little room,
he's finally got his hands on that
priceless ancient artifact
and he's about to make a break for it
when the great stone walls start closing in
from all sides,
add snakes
or spiders
for dramatic effect.

that's how it feels sometimes
getting older.

there are these terrible things
like bills,
interest rates,
a body past its prime,
rotting and wrinkling
and wearing out.
the expectations
the responsibilities,
past due
penalty fees
and fines.

even if you manage to escape
the shrinking
snake filled
deathtrap

there's sure to be some
massive stone ball
rolling
unstoppable
right behind you.

and now it's time
for those weak old knees to run.

you may make it out alive this time,
but there's always a sequel in the works.

Son Of A Ghost

I met my father recently,
and we tried to make a connection.

I needed to know
where I came from,
I felt like I needed to know
what to say to my kids someday
if they asked about their Grandpa.

he was sick,
his days were running out.

as it happened
I was ashamed to be his son
and he
was ashamed to be my dad.

I had just enough time to find out
why I was better off without him.

The Girl At The Creekside Inn

did you hear?

a little crowd formed on the footbridge
moms were blocking little eyes from seeing
cops were pleading with everyone,
please – keep moving
there is nothing to see
nothing you want to see.

she was only twenty years old
and there they were
pulling her crumpled, barely used
corpse
out from a crack between some huge boulders
on the bank of the creek.

if she were alive
she couldn't have pushed herself into that little space
she must have just kind of
settled in there…

had to have been raped
kidnapped or got too drunk
fell from something
hit her head…

turned out worse,
it's heavier on the heart
when its not an accident
or some monstrous crime.

this was something
she chose.

shot herself with her father's gun.

she left her family's house,
she was missing on her birthday.

she checked herself into a lonely room
at the old Creekside Inn.

who knows
what went through her mind
who knows
what could have happened
if she had just reached out
cried out
if she had just said something
or called someone.

she spent her last night
completely alone
in that room.

she took a shower.

she watched some late night television
and then she fell asleep.

early in the morning
she took a walk along the water,
she enjoyed the sun,
took her socks off
dipped her feet

in the cool water,
clean and calm

running

forever.

Not Surprised Anymore
When I Let Myself Down

so many times
I've thought
this is it

things are really gonna turn around
shit is changing
from this moment on
I'm gonna be better
from here on out

starting today
I'm a better person
I'm pulling myself
out of the shit
and I'm cleaning up
I'm gonna answer my phone
when a friend calls
I'm going I keep my house up
I'm gonna do what I gotta do

starting right this second
I'm a new man.

I've smoked so many
last cigarettes ever

Deathbed In My Head

can't help wondering
if he felt ready
when death came to him.

they had him locked down
tied to a bed,
chained up like a criminal...

there were machines to the left
and machines to the right
machines standing guard,
pumping shit in
and sucking shit out.

I wonder how he felt,
I wonder if he knew who he was.

I want my head clear,
I want my memories
all of them
the horrible and the highlight reel.

I want to feel my death
the way I felt my life
from my first fuck
up to the last time I made love.

Flat Tire

I was on a plane
flying to the city
and I overheard an old man
in the row behind me
telling a story
to the stranger beside him.

it was a story about his little girl
and how she passed away.

he said it happened on her seventh birthday.
they were walking together,
they were holding hands
on their way to a toy store.

he said
they did this every year,
they walked to the toy store
and she would choose a present,
and each year she'd ask,
"anything in the store, papa?
anything?"

and
he'd say
"anything in the store
for my baby."

I twisted my neck and I
shifted in my seat so I could look back,
so I could see them between the seats.

then his voice crumbled
under the weight
of his memories
and his chin dimpled up
like a golf ball.

then the old man began to cry.

I admire that ability some people have
to just be so emotionally honest
in front of strangers.

the woman sitting next to the old man
told him it was okay,
he should just rest and that he didn't have to finish the
story.

"I'm sorry"
he said between sniffles and
blows into a tissue,
"but if you don't mind,
I need to finish telling you this."

the old man had stopped crying,
he was resting his chin on his hand
for a long minute as
he watched the clouds dance past his window.

then he sighed
and picked up the story where he'd left off...

"she ran,"
he said,
"before I knew it
her hand had left mine

and then
she was gone."

the woman beside him asked where his daughter went.

and very quietly into his hands he said
that it happened too fast.

he said that just a few days before it happened
he was driving her to school
and she pointed to a car
pulled over on the side of the road,
she asked howcome that car wasn't moving,
why was it stopped?

"I don't know for sure honey,
maybe the car has a flat tire."

then she asked how tires got flat.

he explained that nails sometimes
ended up in the road
and every once in a while
a car runs over a nail
and the tire gets popped
and all the air comes out…

then his little girl asked
why there weren't any vacuum trucks
or like
sweeping robots to make sure all the nails got picked up
so that no cars would get flat tires.

he told her
that was a really great idea
and that they'd write it down

in a letter to the mayor
and they'd both sign their names
and mail it off to city hall.

but before they had a chance to write that letter
his little girl was gone.

seven years old,
walking to the toy store
when she saw a nail
shiny in the road,
she let go of her father's hand
and ran into the street
to pick it up.

the woman in the seat next to him said,
"oh my gawd,
I am so sorry for your loss."

and then he said to her,
"God? no.
there is no god.
there just can not be."

she gasped
and she shook her head

as if she could shake off the evil words
before they stuck to her.

the stupid woman was growing so upset
the flight attendant had to come shuffling over
to check on her.

the man looked out the window again,
watching the dancing clouds…

then he smiled at his reflection in the glass.

I think he smiled
because he knew better than anyone
how to carry on.

Quitter

I fell asleep and saw
the silliest things
I got all caught up
in a rock 'n roll dream.

I couldn't see
how childish I was being
to think
I was born
to win the lottery.

I took the future
from right in front of me
and I handed it all off to the company,
but after all those years
of backing down,
my eyes are open.

so call the stuffed suits
in sales and marketing,
round them up,
have a fucking meeting
let them know
they can stop now,
they can quit wasting money on me.

Like A License To Stay Hopeless

it's not like
one day
everything just
snaps
into place
and makes perfect
sense.

no matter what you and I do
first thing this morning
someone somewhere
is gonna kill someone
for something.

that won't change,
what's happening everywhere,
here and there.

come on,
let's not be stupid.

it's not like
everything's gonna
snap into place.

To Cut
A Me Shaped
Hole In Time

I saw myself.

it was me
doing all those
fucking terrible things
and I think I tried to do something about it,
but I couldn't make him stop.

he lied.

he cheated and he stole,
killed,
he raped and searched for more
shit to break.

I stood by
watching
helpless
useless
stupid
fuck

it stands to reason
that if any one of us,
you,
me,
our mothers and our friends –
if we closed our eyes

and went back some years
we could each see similar things.

none of us
can do anything now
to change the past.

in that respect
I guess
we're all on level ground.

Oh, Hell

if you
or anyone else knew
the kinds of things I think about,
the kinds of things I do.

damned to a hell
I don't even believe in.

it's alive
I'm dead
and it's hot
all the time.

Train Song

years ago
a friend of mine
packed a small bag of clothes,
grew himself a beard
and took to the streets
where he'd beg all day for coins,
smoke the last bits of
cigarettes from the trash bins
behind restaurants.

he had a scholarship
to a great school
but that would just mean
a life of corporate slavery,
working his fingers to the bone
behind a desk
in some high rise filing cabinet
for zombies.

we lost touch over the summer
the way we all seem to spread out
after school got through
we drifted apart – chasing money
chasing dreams
in different directions
until the things we once shared
like the little rubber bands binding us together

just snapped.

I ran into him on the train
and he sang me a beautiful song
about the way the sun
is the same sun
that rises every single day
and for that very reason
the spirit in him
was each morning
brand new.

A Fucking +

I heard this story about a kid in art school.

he did a sort of
performance piece
for his final project.

everybody packed into the corner
of a downtown gallery,
they crowded around
a stool with a revolver sitting on it,
and a bullet beside it.

that's it.

a single bullet
standing up
next to a gun
laying down.

that's it.

and the crowd was in love.

brilliant,
they said to each another,
brilliant.

but then the door of the gallery swung open
and the artist strode across the room,
shouldered his way through the crowd.

he said nothing,
just picked up the pistol off the stool,
then he picked up the bullet
and stuck it in the gun,
spun his chances once,
held the pistol up to the side of his head
and before anyone could do anything to stop him,
he pulled the trigger
and he put the gun back down on the stool
and he left the room.

To Call It An Argument Implies At Least One Of Us Was Listening

"believing something
because it feels good
doesn't make it so.
it doesn't make it real.
sorry."

I said,
maybe for the fifth time
in that
conversation.

then she said something like,
"but what's the point of living
if there's no heaven
after everything in this
horrible hell on earth?"

she said,
"I want to believe in heaven.
I want to believe in god.
I want to think I'm going somewhere nice
when I die..."

my jaw clenched shut hard.

I wanted to scream.

"believing in something

because it feels good
doesn't make it real."

I said again…

that's six.

"look," I said,
"if you think you need a god
to give you a reason to live,
well
I think that's just about
the saddest thing
I have ever heard."

we looked at each other
and for a moment
each was probably thinking
almost the same thing about the other.

poor
poor lonely soul.

you just don't know any better, do you?

then I changed the subject to something I saw on TV…

talking to people like this
is like digging a hole
in dry sand.

Father's Day

I've lived this whole life
wondering who fucked my mom
way back when.

what's he like?

how might I be like him?

would we share a sense of humor?

would we have the same
secret love of sports?

would we both like guns
and
love art?

could we be free thinking weirdos together?

I hoped all that shit
but I always had something different
 in the back of my mind.

I knew the truth,
so I was always
so afraid
to know him.

what if he was a disappointment?

oh
for fuck's sake
if he apologized for everything?

what if he knew Jesus?

what if he was one of those right wing
crazies?

and of course
he was
all of that.

I'm glad I know for sure now.

in our last exchange of letters
he said
he was ashamed to have me as a son,
I should grow up
and get over it.

he was gone my whole life,
sure,
but there's nothing he could do now
to make it right.

so grow up,
he said,
and be a man.

well...

I know you think you're a man
because you went to
Vietnam and fought a war,

I get that,
but your purple heart
has nothing
to do with
mine.

I said he shouldn't tell me
what it means to be a man…

a man raises his fucking kids.

It's Not Empty Or Pointless

the point is
you make your own point.

and that
is so gorgeous a vision
to know
you were born into a confusing world
and you make of it what you can

and then
as quickly as it started
it's over.

some people get more chances
some people get more breaks
some people get more days to play the game
and some people get less.

I hope you get as many as you want.
I hope you get as much of
whatever it is you want.

so,
make love while you can
and laugh when you have to.

sometimes there's no other way
to get by.

Eternal Suckerpunch
And A Dog Toy For A Nose

like one of those little dog toys
my nose whistles when I breathe in
and a different note
when I breathe out.

allergies,
congestion,
suckerpunched
when I was a teenager.

it was a fight over a girl.
I thought I was gonna marry her
someday
when we were both through with school.

I passed up an art school scholarship
because I couldn't imagine leaving her,
I got her name tattooed on my arm,
just to cover it up
eventually.

anyway
I was on a skateboard
flying like a bat out of hell
when a friend of mine
who had been fucking this girl
behind my back,
he decided to pop out from behind a wall
and crack me in the nose.

and so
years after those friendships
and our triangle with the girl
and the tattoo
is all blacked out and hidden forever,
there's still my crooked nose
whistling a sad,
very boring song.

A Stranger In The Mirror

fuck.

almost every morning
it's the first word out of my mouth.

then I hold a little pill
in the palm of my left hand.

I swear at it too.
and fuck you.

swallow it
so I can handle another day.

I'm not one for complaining,
who am I kidding?
it's all I know how to do.
and I feel like a used up whore
sitting on an old man's lap,
gotta be more to life than this.

I know there is
but I'm not so sure how to get it.

who is that

motherfucker in the mirror?

it's a stranger.

what does he want from me?

I leave him
stranded when I walk away.

I'm sure I will never know.

Take The Tracks

his great grandfather
parked his car on the tracks
and waited in there
for a train.

and his granddad worked in the trainyards.

when he was a kid
he thought granddad did something with bombs
and the army or the navy or something,
thought
during the big war
he was loading up
bombs to be taken far away
and dropped on people's heads.

turns out he just drove around
in a company truck
checking the cargo
in each of the train cars.

he was always fond of trains.

like a symbol
of the past
of strength.

regardless of the destination
each and every track
leads straight to the horizon.

Kinda Hard To Say Lonely

music in my ear
it isn't
gossip at some bar.

it isn't looking for a back to use
to warm up a knife,
it's a friend.

the music exists for me
when I need it
and goes away when I don't.

stories I read,
they give me
their honest and
full attention
and I return the favor.

easy friends
pages,
songs.

give so much and take nothing away.

Free Will And The God Bomb

well here I was in the middle of another
silly argument about god
and I was trying to get an answer
about the concept of free will.

I asked if god knows everything.

well of course he does.

and I asked
if he had any sort of plan
for how the world would end.

well
of course he does.

I wondered
how far
my own free will
could take me
before the big referee
would blow his big whistle
and call the foul.

I asked
what would happen
if I had managed to engineer some
ghastly new super weapon,
something so powerful

all I'd have to do is say the word
and I could blow this whole place up.

if I had this thing
all ready to go
and I could wipe us all out
with the push of a button,
messing up god's whole party plan,
would he stop me?
or would he honor his promise
of a fate beyond his influence,
would I still be granted
freedom of will?

Fire And Clouds

I love lots of
people who believe in god.
I guess something like nine out of ten
of the people I interact with on a daily basis
believe in heaven,
they think they're going to go there when they die
and
if they know how I think,
that I don't buy any of it,
they'd believe that I'm gonna burn in hell
when I die.

I'm able to respect these people
and leave them to their stories…

I wish they could see things my way,
but I know they never will
and I can't change that.

so all I'm left with
is the respect I have for the right
of a person
to make their own decisions
about what's real and right.

but
it's really hard for me to believe
that someone who thinks I'm living wrong,
that someone who thinks they're living right,

that someone who thinks they've got a relationship
with the inventor of everything,
it's hard for me to believe they're capable of
truly respecting me.

how could they see me as an equal
when they see themselves in the clouds
and me in the fire.

Every Morning Is Goodbye

I watched
for one
short and terrible moment
through the window of a city train
as a workman in a basket
on the end of the arm of a crane
was changing a light bulb or something
in a traffic signal,
he must have leaned too far
or someone moved the crane arm
when they shouldn't have,
I'm not sure what happened
but the basket just tipped him out
and he fell down to the street below.

and when I saw that vivid red
painting the street beneath his hard hat,
I hoped he kissed his wife
before he left for work
that morning.

Luggage

I wonder about my last words.

whenever I say them.

will they be
something like

I haven't said enough,
so much left…

or

it's all regret,
I'm so sorry,
I've said way too much.

a list of my
defeats,
I list of ways I failed.

a list of my accomplishments,
could anything,
in the end
really feel like a victory?

I can only hope.

there were times when I vanished,
ran away when I was needed
by people who loved me.

there were times I stayed too long,
wore my welcome thin.

there were words
that hurt,
words I never meant to say,
I was so good at escaping.

might my dying lips
be too weak to keep my secrets
from running free?

there were words I had to say,
should have said
to make things better,
I'll take so many with me.

Don't Know Where To Go

I just watched my feet this time
walking along the thin ledge,
I saw cars blurring beneath me.

seems like everything
is getting squished through
some invisible force field
before it gets to me.

my own thoughts
are anything but mine.

can't be
if they hurt like this.

a bright, sunny day
is a sky full of clouds
in my view.

like something in my head
is taking everything,
making it look and sound
and smell like shit
shit shit
before I get to it.

ruined
before it gets to me.

I need a room

full of nothing but pillows
and some time
to figure this out.

Paper Airplane

it got to the point
where I was dreaming like this
every night

being free of gravity
and guilt
and everything.

there I am
writing on the wing
of a paper airplane -

I will miss you too

step out onto the balcony,
climbing the over the railing.

I look back inside
at the airplane on the table...

I check the time
so I know my time,
so I choose my time.

and then
floating
on a journey
to forever
and the city street
below.

Surviving Is Easy

don't get down,
look at your life,
you've got a car that runs
a beautiful wife
money comes to you easily,
thanks – fortune cookie,
you're important to a lot of people.

you've got friends,
people think you're funny,
they ask you where you buy your clothes.

you've signed autographs,
I've never been asked to sign an autograph,
look at your life.

life is beautiful,
the sun is shining!
thanks,
fuckin' greeting card,
hippie bumper sticker,
have a nice day.

snap out of it.

snap out of it.

snap out of it.

man, if I could snap out of it

don't you think I would?

people don't snap out of
stomach cancer,
they don't snap out of
male pattern baldness,
sorry,
I can't snap out of this.

Just Us Again

we held each other tightly
and I said,
"we used to have these magical hugs,
when everything else would disappear,
the world would go away.
now when I hold you,
I feel like you're just
waiting for me to let go...

I want us
to have those hugs again."

and then I realized
we were having
one of those magical hugs
for the first time in a while...

we can do this.

we can make it.

we are still
in love.

Visitor

I've tried to explain
the way it feels
when I know a bad, dark period is about to start.

it's not exactly like a dark cloud
on the horizon,
it's more like
when you're walking
on a sidewalk
down a dark city street,
and you see a figure up ahead,
something about the body language
something about the posture
just a little feeling says
this guy's bad…

so you cross the street
and try to avoid him

but he stops to light a cigarette,
leaning on a post until you pass him by.

then,
just like you expect,
just what you're afraid of,
he crosses the street and starts to follow you.

he follows you all the way to your house
and you go inside,
you close the door,

and just like you expect,
just what you're afraid of,
he knocks on the door.

he's going to come in
one way or another.

there's no reasoning with him.

so you let him in
and he takes a seat.

and you're either going to give him what he wants,
which usually means
you're going to hurt yourself,
or you find a way
to either entertain him
or ignore him
until he decides it's time
to stand up
and walk out the door.

that's what it's like,
you're mostly helpless,
paralyzed with fear
of what he might make you do.

he always ends up leaving
and you know you'll see him again
out there on the streets
you just have to find a way
to make him leave
without taking you with him.

Too Safe

today I had a long talk
with a really strange friend of mine.

he says he's taken up a new hobby,
and I'm thinking
bike riding, painting, pulling weeds out in the garden...

he said
"I'm not sure what it is, man. I think about it all day,
then I get off work
and I gotta go do it somewhere
I gotta find someplace new,
it's not the same as doing it at home,
that's nowhere near as exciting."

and I said, "so you mean to tell me
you could wait until you're safe at home
but instead, you jack off in coffee shop bathrooms?"

"Not just coffee shops, man!"

he said,

"I jack off in movie theaters
and restaurant bathrooms,
one time I did it when I was waiting for my doctor
to come back into the little room, you know?
nurse says to take off my clothes and the next thing I know
I've got a hard cock and I just start going at it!"

he lifted his head
and kinda stared through me for a second,
he scratched his head
trying to remember all the other places
he had done this.

"umm, where else, I know there's more," he said.

I told him he was insane.
people go to prison for that.
it's not safe.

he straightened up in his seat,
"I hit the library the other day,
I haven't been in there in years,
I think the smells got me going,
nostalgia."

I couldn't believe it,
I mean, I believed it
but I couldn't believe it.

I told him he should be careful
people are crazy,
someone might hear him talking this way,
just wait for him to go to the bathroom
and call the cops.

he said,
"listen, do I fuck little kids, man? – no, I don't,
I'm not hurting anybody."

he started getting loud
making big motions with his arms.

I wasn't arguing,

just looking out for him.

"don't knock it 'til you try it, man!"

I told him I wasn't gonna try it.
I knew I was though.
I agreed with everything he was saying.
what a thrill it would be,
see a hot girl
serving coffee or
telling me to get my clothes off at the doctor's office
I knew exactly what he was saying.

"don't you get it?" he went on,
"you said the magic word a minute ago –
SAFE – who wants to be safe?
safe fuckin sucks,
safe is boring,
fucking is boring too,
because it's safe
you're not gonna get in trouble
for fucking…"

we both paused a minute,
I was thinking of all the ways
you really could get in trouble fucking,
I assume he was thinking the same thing,
but we let it slide,
he said, "if I get arrested for jerkin' it somewhere man,
I'm gonna jack off at the police station too!"

I laughed loud and hard
because I knew he wasn't kidding.

"ooh, what about a church?" I asked.

"oh shit, yeah... that sounds like one for you, man."

I laughed again
loud and hard
because I knew
he was right.

Sad Face Stuck Like That

let's look forward to what's coming next.

I know we've worked things
a certain way
for what seems like forever
but it's time to change it up.

can we change the default settings
and make it so the first expression of the day
is something other than a frown?

it's like how people always tell their kids,
keep making that silly face
and one of these days
it's gonna freeze
and stay that way forever.

seems to be the truth
with these
upside down smiles of ours.

the more I dwell on low points
the higher the flood waters rise.

Seven Years Into The Rest Of Our Lives

I wonder lately
if I still make her happy.

I've been so hard to love
and I usually feel like a burden.

just enough weight
at the bottom of a ribbon
to keep that heart shaped balloon
from flying high as it wants.

I wake up early enough sometimes
to see her smiling in her sleep,
so I lay there
and I wait until the alarm goes off,
when she wakes up,
her smile goes away.

sometimes her eyes open
and see me.

I wonder how that feels.

did I trick her into
a life of raising a baby
that will never grow up?

did I sell her something
she didn't want?

is she more comfortable
than discontent,
heels just deep enough in the dirt
that she's willing to ride it out,
or does she still
love me
the way she did
before she knew me
so well?

I sometimes wish
I could make her forget
who I am.

By Starlight

this ship is being blown by the wind
and I'm not sure where it's going
but maybe I don't need to know.

what if I'm not the captain?

this would be so much easier
if I were just a passenger,
not my job to know
anything.

I could be fussing over all the math
and the maps
and navigating by stars...

or
maybe these stars
are just pretty things to look at,
on my way to wherever I'm going.

bottom of the sea.

A Fish You Won't Catch Again

I was bored of this
before you were even born.

I was moving on
while you
were just moving in.

I remember that
brand new buzz
like it was yesterday.

but it was not
yesterday.

it was a long time ago.

that feeling
is a fish
that I will never
catch again.

Rusty Rollercoaster

get me off this thing
piece of shit
rusty old carnival ride

the bolts holding us up here
are rotting more
with each season
come and gone
sea air salt decay.

the guy down there
running the whole thing
pushing buttons
and twisting
the cap off of his whiskey
looks like he's fallen asleep at the wheel
of this massive death machine.

gotta keep my balance,
even though I'm sitting down
I try to look at the same bright star in the sky
as it passes by
with each nauseating
round trip.

when we were kids
we use to laugh at the old people
hunched over
throwing up into trash cans
but now it's us
asking our friends to hold our ice cream cones
while we puke.

that's what you pay for.

the stomach ache,
the spinning head,
get back in line
do it again.

It Happens To Other People, Not Us

we each took turns
jumping from the roof
into the swimming pool
until that weird minute of silence
while a red cloud
spread its spidery legs
from the deep end to the steps.

we put our nickels and our pennies
on the tracks
waiting for that great big train
to blow through our town,
east to west
until that day
when the train took the red-headed kid
and splashed his freckles
from here to the coast.

we dressed in all black clothes
and we robbed parked cars,
opened every unlocked door
and filled our backpacks with
cigarettes and CDs,
stereos and shit,
until someone came sneaking up behind
and swung an aluminum baseball bat
at the youngest kid in our group,
he was just our lookout
posted in the parking lot,
least guilty of the bunch,
we heard the ping
just like if he was
hitting a baseball with that bat.

we drank like we were invincible
on the weekends
and when the summertime came
we drank even more
and we ate pills
and we snorted whatever we could
every night.

one kid went to the hospital
to get her stomach pumped.

one kid went to the hospital
to fix a great big deep hole
that his buddy made in his back
with an expensive
Japanese filet knife.

two kids left the party
not knowing
they were soon to be
mommy and daddy,
congratulations!

show must go on.

one kid was on acid or mushrooms
and he was entertaining everyone all night
he was hilarious
and at around three in the morning
he called everyone into the kitchen
so they could all see him eat dynamite!
of course we all assumed he
was going to chug some hot sauce
or eat a crazy killer chili pepper,
we expected something silly,
but nobody thought he was going to
light the fuse
on a massive firecracker
and swallow it.

but that's what he did.

maybe the fuse was supposed to go out
when it got in his mouth,
maybe he was just a stupid kid on drugs,
grew up on cartoons.

but in the cartoons it never went,
everyone gather around
watch me bleed from my nose and eyes.

at least someone
had the sense
to put a pillow
under his head
while he twitched
on the kitchen floor.

If I'm Still Right Here Tomorrow

I am scared.

I wonder if I can live

with these pictures
in my head.

I close my eyes
and I see you.

tears coming out
so fast and so hard,
if you cried a thousand years
these tears
would carve canyons.

I am scared.

I wonder if I can live
knowing
what kind of monster I am,
if I can survive
much longer
knowing
I am a fucking liar.

the secret is out,
the mask is off.

I am everything I have always pretended not to be.

I don't deserve
love

but if I can show my ugly side,
would I have a choice?

or would I have to leave?

I am scared
because I know myself
too well.

I know I will always
destroy
what I need most.

I will always
falter when
sure footing is
the only way through.

I am scared.

I will always
be cursed this way,
to be lost forever,
no compass
no conscience
no honor
and no clear path.

I hurt the people I love.

I love
the people
I hurt.

I am so scared.

and when I fall asleep
I'm scared I might wake up
and still be me.

this
same
defeated,
broken me,
just garbage in that bed.

and when you wake up,
from the nightmare
so many years long,
the nightmare I am,
the horror of trying to love me,
could you be relieved
to know

I'm gone?

it's finally
over...

I'm so fucking scared.

Until The Crowd Goes Home

you never know
how well things work
until they break.

knees and elbows,
they used to do their jobs in silence
and they bent so smooth,
now the old machine is falling into disrepair.

sick old robot joints need grease

you think the files
are all in proper order
until the day you realize
you've been forgetting little details
phone numbers and names
of used up friends and former lovers.

Sunday Monday Tuesday
may as well
share a square
on the calendar,
it's all the same

of course
the hair will fall out
the belly and the ass will grow,
ladies, you'll get fat ankles too –
the eyes will go from bright to lazy
the ears will grow hair in them
and they'll hear less,

mine will sing a high pitched one-note song
forever
ringing, ringing, nobody home.

the feet will ache
in line for carnival rides and movie theaters
excitement
the old heart can hardly handle
hope for a heart attack,
something quick.

god damn it
the back will twist
disfigured
trying to hold the rest of the mess up
until the day it falls down.

you sure there's a point to all of this?

one day they stop calling you man,
bro, dude,
and they say sir…

girls,
you'll hate ma'am.

we wont get by on our looks
anymore
who knows how much we ever really did….

start big
end small

save your best tune
for the encore

unless of course,
the crowd just goes home
before you've played your last number.

rather than stomping feet
and clapping hands
whistles and cheering,
they're hailing taxi cabs
for a ride to the rest of the night.

rest of the night for you is just that,
rest.

you gave it up so long ago
fruitless search for meaning.

Bridges

I'll tell this story
maybe it'll help.
help me,
help you,
I don't know.

I was in a tailspin.

I was in a darker place
than I had ever been
and I was waiting
for January third to come around.

it's the day I was born,
it was the right day to die.

I had my plan
I had a spot picked on the bridge.

it was November
or December,
I think it was both.

a long time to feel this way.

it didn't matter
how well things were going for me,
didn't matter if I was doing
some of my best work of my life.

it didn't matter if my friends loved me.

it didn't matter if I had
a love that made people jealous,
it didn't matter.
nothing could.

I hadn't cried for myself in a long time.
I really just stopped caring,
I let it beat me.

so I started drinking again,
I started smoking again,
I swallowed whatever pills people handed me,
I spent money I didn't have
on things I didn't need.

I'll tell this story,
maybe it will help.

I had blackouts
and panics I hoped might kill me,
out of my head
so maybe
guilt wouldn't be the last thing I felt.

growing up I thought the most important thing
I could do
would be to make things
art, songs, whatever, just make things
that might make other people happy.

if the things I made
and the things I said
made people like me,
maybe I could matter so much to so many people

that eventually
I might matter to myself.

but all this time,
I believed something
that would never be true.

you people
can't save me.

and you shouldn't have to,
it's not your job.

it's my job
to care enough about my own life
to keep going.

well,
I'm no good at that job.
I was failing.

I was done.

I knew killing myself,
fuck – those two words together
just make it sound so selfish -
I knew choosing my time to die
would leave big holes
in a lot of hearts,
hearts I care so deeply for,
but I felt like they would eventually move on,
they'd heal up
and in the long run
it would be easier on them;
remembering me,
going through the grief,

then getting better
and living the rest of their lives
lighter,
more free
than they are now with the weight
of dealing with me...

you know when you get really drunk
and you do a bunch of stupid shit,
then the next day your friends start telling you
about all the silly things you did and said,
and you don't remember any of it?

that's what this was like
for a few days here
a couple of weeks there...

I knew when I was going to die,
so I didn't care who I hurt
what I broke on my way out the door.

I do remember some conversations I had
with strangers
and with some friends.

of course when I spoke to friends about how I was feeling
I watered it down
I lied,
I put a candy shell over everything,
like it was gonna get better
like I was just feeling down,
but that everything would turn around,
I could feel it.

when I talked to strangers about it

I was more honest
than I could ever be
with people who really cared about me.

I told them
I saw this as the most logical
most noble way
to walk away.
it was my life,
and it was my right to end it,
instead of going though these ups and downs,
I couldn't do it anymore,
the extremes were just getting so much worse now.

when I was a kid I'd get depressed
and that's when I would write a song
or I'd paint.

and I'd do some drugs
and soon
everything would feel okay again.

As I got older
I'd lie my way out of depressions,
masking it,
hiding the true darkness
that was taking over,
all I could do was hope
I could keep up the bullshit
until the urge to die
went away.

this time was so different.

I would go from feeling
like superman
to feeling completely hopeless
and back again,
more difficult each time.

I'm telling this story
hoping
it might help
me.

I went to a club
to see a band
and hang out with some friends.

Sarah and our friend,
they knew something wasn't right,
when I refused to drive
saying I was planning on drinking a lot.

any time someone who doesn't drink for a few years
starts up again,
it's only a matter of time before
it gets out of control.

earlier in the day
while she was at work
I ate a few pills and tried to write,
of course
nothing came out.

it's not like it was when I was a kid,
my depressions weren't pushed out
with a pen anymore,
they were so much bigger
and heavier now,
so I ate more pills.

before she came home I checked my eyes in the mirror,
when I eat too many of these
my eyes get weird and dark,
it's strange,
they seem to change from their greenish color
to a dull brown
when I'm high
or when I'm really low,
when I'm really not myself.

whoever that is.

I thought I looked alright in the mirror,
so I pretended I was fine
and we went out.

I ate some other pills in the car on the way to the club.

this isn't some rockstar story glorifying drugs,
like something to make myself seem cool,
but it's definitely,
unfortunately,
a cliché.

we got to the club and I headed straight for the bar.

I've always been a lightweight drunk

a cheap date,
I don't need more than four beers to get fucked up,
so, this night
I remember maybe my sixth beer,
then the rest starts to fade into the fog.

Sarah and our friend were having fun watching the band
and I was on a mission.

this could be
how I die,
at least I might not seem like I did it on purpose -
if I died that night from all these pills and drinks,
maybe she'd think
it was accidental.

I can't imagine
what she'd feel,
knowing I killed myself,
like if it was somehow her fault,
but nobody would blame themselves for an accident.

this is just what I've managed to piece together
in the months that have passed.

I remember telling someone secrets,
nothing huge, I don't think,
just things I'd felt were weighing me down.
things I'd never said out loud before.

I talked about wanting to give up and about
times I had cheated and hurt people,
disappointed myself...
I did grow up
around Catholics
so maybe this was my last confession?

I do remember one moment
very clearly
when a girl I was drinking with
handed me two pills,
I didn't know what they were
and I didn't care.

I just swallowed them,
now there were pills of at least three different kinds
swimming in my guts
mixing with the alcohol
and my blood
and excuses,
I think I remember that moment clearly
because I knew it was
what would push my body over the edge.
I remember the moment when I was sure
I had enough mixed up in me to do the job.

who knows what happened for the next
hour or two,
I was gone.
gone.

I vaguely remember walking to the car,
I know I was sitting in the front seat,
then I remember pushing the button
to roll down the window,
we were on the freeway.
it was so dark.

the last thing I remember
was the vomit coming out of my mouth...
it looked like smoke,
it moved in slow motion,
spider webs,

a white silk scarf,
a ghost
silent from my mouth
to the window
and out.

now
my eyes were
open
but I saw nothing.

just black.

just
black.

she told me the next day about how
they had pulled the car over in the woods
and I was standing,
throwing up on myself,
trying to talk
but no real words coming out –
then when they tried to put me back in the car
I stiffened up
and my eyes rolled back in my head.

they had to put me in the back of the car
like a long piece of wood.

they didn't know I was dying.
they didn't know about the pills.

they knew it didn't take much to get me drunk
and they knew I drank a lot,
but they didn't know about all the pills.

I found out later,
all this throwing up
probably saved my life.

even later
I realized
this puking fit
ruined my plans.

no easy way out for me.
next stop, January third.

the next few days are a blur to me now,
I know I was talking about
wanting to fuck other people,
I was talking about how
I wasn't who I thought I'd be by now,
I said I was done,
I was tired of being a burden.
that's all I've ever been to anyone
all my life
a weight
for other people to carry around,
a weight
that keeps everyone else
on the ground
when that's not where they deserve to be,
I was the reason
she wasn't an actress
I was the reason
we'd never have enough money
to be comfortable,
I was the shit
standing between this rut
and a happy future.

I'm telling this story,
not sure why...
maybe to help myself.

when I was a kid,
I was a burden on my family.

and when you're a kid
and you feel like the best thing
for everyone
would be to take yourself
out of the equation
you pack a bag
and you run away from home.

as a grown up
the way I see myself
making it easier for everyone,
the way I can help
is to take myself out of the equation.

as an adult
you don't just pack a bag and run away.
you have to really disappear forever.
and sure,
people will cry for a while.

they'll have a barbeque on the anniversary of your death
and they'll all stand in little groups around a fire
smoking cigarettes and saying things like,

"I still can't believe he's gone."
or,
"I keep expecting him to walk through that door."
and
"this is so weird,

but I'm getting by."
someone will add,

not getting over it,
"I'm I'll never get over it,
but I'm moving on with my life finally."

someone else will say,
"fuck him. I'm still so mad at him for leaving me."

I know this because I've been to a lot of these
memorials,
I've heard all these conversations and I've imagined
all these things being said about me.
they'll hurt for a while, but they'll move on without me.

I'm telling this story and I'm not sure why,
or if I should keep going.

in the days following my pills and drinks night
I am not sure what I said
to her
or to my friends.
I know the types of things I said
but I can't remember specific conversations,
all I have to remember this period of time,
I can't even really think of it as time,
it was a place,
or a monster,
but not time…

all I have to remember this now
are the photos I took
when we went to a park
and tried so hard to play -
like kids.

and
I just kept holding her.

I watched her on a rope swing,
I shot a photo.

I found a dead cat,
I shot a photo.

I touched it with my bare hand,
moved some leaves off its eyes,
and I shot another photo.

I remember feeling
almost jealous
of this dead cat.

he got to be done.
he made it.

I held her again
for a long hug,
I'm sure she felt something strange about it.
I wondered if it might be the last time we touched.

I was asking weird things like
"are we just roommates?"
I said we got along so well,
like best friends,
but were we still lovers?
was I a burden on her?

there are come hot couples
friends of ours
who are always asking us
if we want to fuck…

a lot of people
have assumed we're wild swingers,
but no –
we've never crossed that line,
because we know there's no going back.

well,
since I was going to die on my birthday
I felt like I deserved to have a few things
I've always wanted
before then.

heroin.
cocaine.
three girls sucking my cock at the same time.

love and sex,
they aren't the same thing, I do remember saying this –
like, if love and sex were the same,
then when I'm out of town for two months
and we're separated,
we're obviously not having sex,
so does that mean we don't love eachother?

these were the types of things I was saying
for I'm not sure how long,
at least three days, maybe a month.

she's tried to ask me
more about the ways I was thinking,
she was scared and confused.
I don't think I was scared by then.
I was just ready to die.
my birthday couldn't come soon enough,
I wanted what that dead cat had,
I wanted to be done, to be free.

we spent hours of walking and talking.
this night
felt like the end of everything.

I told her about all the pills I took the night we went out.

she said she knew there had to be an explanation,
that was so much more intense than a regular
night of drinking too much.

it was near Christmas,
so we strolled the rich neighborhood
with the most elaborate decorations,
I snapped more photos,
I look at one she shot of me now,
spreading my arms in front of this
huge lit up reindeer in someone's front yard,
I hardly recognize myself.

we got home
and there was music playing loud,
sometimes we'd leave it on
for the dogs to listen to
when we're gone ...

Joy Division.

I headed straight for the bathroom
to take a shit
and I locked the door...

it's a habit leftover from being in a band on tour,
because
you're never shitting in your own bathroom
when you're on the road.

I think I'm telling this story
to help her.
to help her understand.

so I was sitting on the toilet
and I heard her phone beep,
she got a text message,
then she started banging on the bathroom door
she was screaming,
she was crying...

she calls me E.

a lot of my closest friends do.

and she was screaming, "EEEEEE!" and crying
and pounding on the door so hard
I could see it cracking up the middle.

I jumped up off the toilet,
and unlocked the door and swung it open.

she collapsed in the hallway
and I picked her up and I asked,
"who died? what happened, who died!?"

we had a string of deaths
over the last couple of years
tragic freak accidents,
suicides, a dead grandpa...
it seemed like another death every couple of months
and most of those times,

when we'd find out someone died,
I'd be in the bathroom
and she'd get a text message or a phone call
then the next thing I know
she's crying at the bathroom door
waiting for me to come out
so she could tell me
and we could cry together.

this time,
she was crying because she thought
I was killing myself in the bathroom.

I wish I knew what I had said in the conversations
leading up to getting home and me
going to take a shit,
I must have worried her so bad
with the things I'd said.

did I tell her I was going to kill myself?
I wish I could remember.

I held her in the hallway
and she was squirming like a dog
who doesn't want to be held.

she couldn't possibly see me through those tears
but she said,
"you need to get help, E,
you need to talk to someone,
I can't do this anymore,
you're scaring me
so bad."

I'm telling this story
and I don't know why.

I don't know anything.

So we called the psychiatry department
of our local hospital.

I don't remember much of the conversation,
but the man on the phone had such a soft
warm voice,
the kind of voice you trust right away.

I remember thinking
it's cool that this guy is in the business
of helping people
instead of selling stuff.

the soft voice asked to speak to Sarah
so I handed the phone over
and she left the room.
I couldn't hear words,
just the notes,
the sad, muffled music of her voice through the door.

a few minutes later she came out
and she said we had an appointment
at the hospital
first thing in the morning.

I don't remember sleeping that night.
but I must have

because I remember waking up.

when we arrived at the adult psychiatry building,
I recognized the voice of the man I spoke to on the phone.

he greeted both of us by name
and he took us to a room where we met his boss,
I can't remember her face now
but I do remember a strange feeling,
I felt like I knew everyone in the building,
all their faces looked familiar and I pointed people out,
"I think I went to school with that guy."

I found out later, this feeling is common
when you're having a mental breakdown.

the boss lady asked me what was going on.

of course, I don't know what I said.

then she asked Sarah what was going on
and Sarah said that I was scaring her.
she said that I was acting strange,
I wasn't myself,
I was talking a lot about dying
and I had overdosed on pills
and alcohol
a couple of days before.

the boss lady,
with her clipboard on her lap...

she asked me,
"Eric, do you have a plan to kill yourself?"

and I said,

"no, not right now, I'm not planning to kill myself."

not now, I thought,
it wasn't even Christmas yet.
I was holding out for my birthday.

of course I didn't say that.
that was the truth
and I wasn't there
to tell the truth.

the lady said,
"that's not what I'm asking you, Eric.
I asked if you have a plan, have you planned
what you would do if you *were* to kill yourself?"

"oh yeah, I'd jump off the Golden Gate bridge." I answered.

I looked at her eyes when I said it.
I wasn't feeling any emotions...

Sarah was sitting in the chair beside me
I remember the sound she made when I said that,
but I don't know how to describe it.

the man with the warm voice asked me
if what happened the other night
with the pills and the drinking,
if that was a suicide attempt...

I said I wasn't trying to kill myself,
I just didn't give a fuck.

and he said that when someone
doesn't give a fuck and they do something like that
it's called a suicide attempt.

"oh," I said.
and I shrugged my shoulders.

I didn't trust the soft voice man anymore.

then the lady asked,
"do you feel safe?"

I said yes.

"right now I feel safe."

"but," she continued, "when you are alone…
when your wife goes to work tomorrow
and you're by yourself,
are you going to be safe?"

now, here's where I made a decision that changed my life.

and you don't get many of these, I don't think…

you don't get many times when you know
you're making a life changing decision.
of course,
you can always trace time back through events
and see how certain choices you made
shaped your future.

but here was one I saw
plain as day.

I knew I could tell this lady
that I felt fine,
I was safe on my own –
and she'd mark something on her clipboard,
probably schedule me a follow-up appointment

and I would make it to January third.

I could still go through with my plan.

or I could tell her the truth.

no, I didn't feel safe.
not there.
not anywhere.
not now
not any time ever.

I wasn't safe from myself today
or tomorrow.

I was fucking terrified.

tormented by my own thoughts,
horrified by being left alone
and knowing I wasn't even
going to be able to make it
from that chair in that office
to Christmas,
to New Year's Eve
or
to my birthday.

this was a life changing decision I was making.

I knew if I said I didn't feel safe
they were going to lock me up.
I knew they couldn't let me walk out of there
if I admitted how I was feeling.

I wanted to keep lying.
would I lie

and keep marching toward my death
or was I going to let these people help me?
help me do what?
keep suffering?
like a brain dead body in a bed,
life support? medication?

I felt my eyes get hot and wet.

I took a short breath,
I was going to say something,
I was going to answer,
but I honestly still don't know what I had decided -

I don't know what I was going to say.

I feel so shitty admitting it now
but I'm pretty sure I was opening my mouth to say,

"I'll be okay by myself tomorrow."

because I remember the image
of the Golden Gate
popping my head
as I shifted in my seat...

I could get out of this room if I just tell them I'm ok...

Sarah was holding my hand.

the man with the soft voice was looking at me.
the lady with the clipboard was looking at me.
I was looking out the window behind them,
everyone was waiting for an answer.

I'm telling this story
hoping it might help you.

"Eric, will you be safe alone?"

before I could say anything,
before I could lie
my tears answered her question for me.

I let out a wail,
chopped up by my shaking body.

I hunched over and my face
landed in my hands.

I was sobbing so hard
and I heard the lady say,
"Eric, what's going to happen now,
it's called the Baker Act,
or a 5150...
do you know what that means?"

I couldn't say anything
but
I managed
to nod my head.

Not Sure
How To Start
A Fire

when I was younger
I was really good
at starting fires.

burning things,
I mean.

I've told you about that before,
little kid
delinquent shit.

then I got a little older
and I got good at
burning bridges.

someday
I might burn my own house down
with my mistakes.

now I wonder
how to start fires
in her heart
if I have to be someone else
to make her love me
like she used to.

Here I'm High Again

today I feel like I can do anything.

but I know
it's not a feeling
that will last long.

I have to try to remember
what this feels like
to be proud
to be hopeful
and to look forward,
from this peak
to the next
overlook the valley.

overlook
the valley.

Didn't Have The Heart
To Cash The Check

I've already seen the other side of it,
the bare walls
behind the posters of my favorite superheroes.
discolored space
tucked safely away
from the sunlight
and cigarette smoke.

I've seen the other sides of things
fantasies and broken wings,
I know the truth and how the whole thing
balances
on a razor thin line
cut deep down to the bone,
a line between a dream come true
and suicide.

I'm still here
talking about it
because
I like to think I never bought into the bullshit,
I never let it buy into me.
because I turned my back
on all the someday money,
mountains of free drugs
homewrecking sex dolls...

I signed my name

but I ended up
growing too fond of my soul
to give it up,
I kept it for myself.

Confession

too much has been done
that you could never
forgive me for.

so much.

I don't know if I could ever
forgive myself.

guilt is in every cell of my body,
it's in my blood now
and it contaminates
all of my thoughts.

you say I am a good man
who's made a few mistakes
and our friends,
they think so much more of me
than I deserve.

I don't know what I'll do
now that I have destroyed
the only
sacred thing in my life.

I have destroyed our love.
it was
the only thing
keeping me alive.

I Know Now

strangers.

they love me
because they don't know me.

my friends
see something
in me
I don't see in myself

but I know
they will be
just fine without me.

I might even serve
as some sort of
inspiration.

or maybe
my name
will be the word
that causes everyone to stiffen up
"I remember this time when Eric...."

and faces will scrunch and quiver
knowing
I'm not coming home this time.

"he wouldn't want us to be sad."

someone might say
between drags off a cigarette.

"he'd hate to see us crying over him."

and that's true...

guys, listen now,
for when
I'm not around to remind you -

you gotta tell a sick joke,
especially when it's an inappropriate moment.

draw a picture of a dick
or a big open butthole
and say it's in my honor.

listen to my songs,
even though I probably hated them in the end,
maybe name a kid after me
and I'll smile proudly at all of you
through the flames of Hell.

As We Move To Be More Temporary

seemed like every year or so
I would have to get a new
bigger box
to hold my growing collection
of photographs.

I saved them all,
blurry shots I thought weren't special
all those years ago,
some are now
all I have left
of dead friends.

Russian Roulette Champion

take a chance
make a change.

I ran full speed
through barbed wire
and made it through
a Russian roulette style
change of moods.

I got my black eye
broken nose
my knocked out tooth.

I'm standing here
on beaten bones
and bruised up knees.

no safety nets.

a Russian roulette style
change of moods.

one in six
one pop
in five little clicks.

Table Saw

my friend's daddy shot himself
out in the garage.

the door that was usually left open
was closed and locked from the inside
and the table saw was running
so that the family in the house
and the rest of the suburbs
wouldn't hear that gun go off.

daddy did it with the shotgun
someone bought for him
for his birthday.

it was the only time
that thing was ever fired.

he planned a couple of hunting trips
with the kids
but always had to cancel last minute
when something big came up
at the office.

he paid off the last of the credit cards,
finally finished painting that fence,
he sold off boxes of comic books
and baseball cards,
old toys and all of that –
and he stuck the money

in a secret savings account,
this was money to put the kids through school.

he put down plastic sheeting
on the floor of the garage,
had a bunch of it left over
from when they painted the baby's room.

it was a hot June afternoon
and daddy's blood
had collected in the corner,
in a pool two inches thick.

how strange it is
that when we lose a lot of blood
and die,
for a short time
that blood on the ground
and on the body
just keeps working,
trying to thicken up
and scab over,
not knowing all that work is pointless.

it had only been an hour or so
when the guy from the house on the corner
came over
and knocked on the front door.

the man
stepped into the living room
and asked if everything was alright.

he said
he thought it was strange

that the table saw
in the garage
had been running continuously
for so long,
but it didn't sound like anyone
was cutting any wood.

everyone just stood still
for what felt like a thousand years,
heads cocked to the side,
listening to the distant sound of that saw.

mom threw her arms up in the air
and said that god
was a heartless monster.

then she
fell to her knees
and threw up on the floor.

Weathervane

she said she had this cloud
in her heart,
something dark and heavy
and she didn't know
what she could do
to clear it out.

she didn't know
how to change the weather in there,
to get happy.

and she told me that she
felt like giving up.

I said I felt the same way
most of the time.

It's What You Hold Onto

sometimes
the most difficult thing
is not
to keep holding on
but to let go.

and you're holding on tight
to a defeated version of yourself.

maybe because you can't let go,
you don't know what will happen.
maybe because
it's just easier to hurt.

but it takes a lot more
energy
and effort
to cry
than it takes to laugh.

or to shrug
to sigh
and keep things
how they are.

View From The Top
Of Shit Mountain

you could climb
and fuck your way
to the top
of a mountain made of shit.

and what would it get you?

nothing but lightheaded
from the thin air.
and your own
hot air.

heart heavy with regret.

no such thing as
friends
up here.

just a short list
of who hates you less.

strangers
down there
with
better things to do than
to be needed
by someone
like me.

Various Cancers, Missteps
And More Bad News

I don't know why
my thoughts turn to death
so often.

my death.
your death.
all of ours.

death is in the footprints behind me.

death is in the sky above.

in the last seconds of a dream
cut off,
interrupted.

death is hanging in the fog above my bed.

until a new day chases it away.

death is in tomorrow
and tonight
if we aren't careful.

yesterday
is black with it
but easy
to avoid.

death is always so busy
searching the space between
the bricks
for a crack
a weak spot
to work on
and take the whole thing
down.

and life,
life is busy
working
hand in hand with death
to keep it
interesting.

Such A Lonely Day

I really do love
my solitary time
but too much of anything
becomes poisonous.

it's one of those days when
I don't bother leaving messages.

the phone rings,
no one picks up.
I hang up.
like I was never there.

my phone rings.
I ignore it.

I go through my list
and call more numbers
but nobody's there.

what would I say?

"hey, it's me... just calling to see how you've been, call me
back."

maybe I've fucked too many people over
or hurt too many feelings

or maybe this is grown up life.

Window Seat

I didn't ride the train every day
but when I did
there was a man who would stand there
on the platform
with his cute young wife by his side
and a beautiful baby
in a stroller...

the man would sip from his coffee cup,
his wife would peck at her blueberry muffin
and both would bend over
to play with the baby
and make baby talk sounds,
then they'd stand up straight again
and kiss each other.

I thought it was adorable.

another great morning
starting another
wonderful day.

then the train would pull up
and the doors would open
and the man would give the wife and baby
a couple more kisses each
then step onto the train
and go straight to a window seat
where he would wave goodbye.

and I'd see the baby giggling
and smiling
as the train took us away,
I could read the wife's lips,
"wave goodbye to daddy!"
and
"we love you!"

everyone else who waited
on the platform
for that train
every day,
we all knew
no matter how full the train might be
when it came,
when those doors opened up,
we always let that man
take his
window seat.

The Couch

there's a couch
out in the middle of a field
at the edge of town,
where I live
and all the neighborhood kids go out there
to waste their time.

generation after generation
of high school slackers,
stoners,
punks and skaters
go out there to the crusty mustard yellow couch
to meet girls and boys from other schools,
to share drugs and trade spit,
to tell stories of the bullies and the jocks,
to make fun of the popular assholes,
they swap phone numbers
they swap girlfriends and boyfriends
and every once in a while
a fight will break out.

for years I've watched them
through a hole in the fence
in my back yard.

I know some of their names,
I know some of their secrets.

I've kept tabs the best I could,

all the little love triangles,
the soap operas
the drama.

I know who's in the closet,
I've seen boys fuck their girlfriends
on that couch
in the afternoon
and then
they're out there
sucking their buddy's cock
later that evening.

I've masturbated
quietly
up against the fence
probably hundreds of times.

a tradition started years ago
where the kids whose senior year was ending
would write their names
and the numbers representing the year of their class
with permanent felt tipped markers
on the arms and the cushions
of the couch.

I don't know who started the ritual,
but it's been going on so long
that there isn't much space left for autographs.

the letters and scribbles
and memories

stand up to a few seasons
before they start to fade away.

it's been so many years now
that I've watched the kids come to the couch
in the first few days of their freshman year,
see them start doing drugs,
and fucking
and fighting
then graduate
and move on
to whatever it is they move on to,
prison
boring desk jobs,
early graves,
marriage and kids of their own.

I don't know where they go
after the couch
but I really enjoy keeping up with them
while I can.

it's kind of like watching television
except less stuff happens.

but when stuff does happen,
since it's real,
it's way more interesting.

watching real stuff happen
through a hole in a fence...

it's much better than
watching fake stuff happen
through a screen.

when I first started watching,
I just stood there in my yard
sometimes for hours
with my hand cupped at my temple,
my left eye squeezed shut,
my legs straining
to keep me up on the tips of my toes.

I'd get really tired
or I'd get hungry
but I would have trouble
pulling myself away from the fence.

the worst part was
when I'd feel a sneeze coming on
or a dry tickle
in the back of my throat.

I learned to suppress coughs
and sneezes
by researching
on military websites
and sniper vet's messageboards,
field handbooks I found at estate sales.

discipline.

I find it fascinating how much control

these snipers have over their bodily functions
nestled in a spot for days.

that was me too,
I was disciplined.

before long
the couch became my biggest obsession
and I started to care more and more
for each year's fresh batch of kids.

there's something special
something so satisfying
about caring for people
who don't even know you exist.

I've been concerned for them
I've cried for them
I've cried with them
and I've gone along with them,
laughing with them
being proud with them.

I've lost jobs for these kids,
I've sacrificed some important relationships
for these kids.

they never knew it
but we had a deal,
as long as they came out to the couch
I'd come to the fence.

then one day I had this great idea!

I went down to the hardware superstore
and I picked out a cheap little tin tool shed
just a little bit bigger
than one of those awful steamy
plastic shit houses they have at the state fair.

I assembled the shed
and I set it up right next to the fence.

I measured some stuff out and I cut a hole
in the wall of the shed
in just the right spot.

I brought a tall bar stool in there
and it was the perfect height
so that I could sit there
all day
and all night,
totally comfortable.

I'd bring my food and water
out to my shed
and I'd bring my blankets
and recently
I brought my little video camera
out to the shed.

god only knows how many times
in the years before I had that camera out there,
I saw things I wished I could
rewind
and watch again and again.

I'm not crazy, you know,

I'm not dumb enough to think what I do is normal.

I can see how some people could think
what I do is sick or wrong or
maybe even illegal,
but one thing I've realized
watching the couch for so long
is that
so-called real friendships
are a lot more difficult to maintain
than my relationship with the kids.

I figure
why fuss with a dialog
when a monolog
is half the trouble?

some people collect stamps
or Star Wars toys,
cooped up all their lives
in their dark houses
with video games
all alone
making love
to pictures on the internet...

that's what some people love.
they love what they love and
I love what I love.

I love watching the couch
and keeping up
with my friends.

say what you want about it,
but these kids never judge me.
I feel safe with them.

I've had so many moments in my shed
I could probably write a whole book
or a movie or something
about all the adventures
and the drama.

but one of the greatest moments
that sticks out in my mind
happened just a couple of months ago.

it was a bright
beautiful morning,
crisp frost crunched in the grass
as the earliest of the early birds arrived
and lit their cigarettes
and when they sat down on the couch
they were horrified to find huge
sticky stains
on the cushions.

thick pools of dark stuff
almost black
right in the center of the couch.

someone choked on a laugh saying
it looked like blood or something
but no,
there was way too much of it to be real.
right?

one of the boys,
my second least favorite
dropped his cigarette when his mouth flopped open,
his lower lip trembled
when it occurred to him...

"it's blood you guys, holy shit! this is *blood*!"

then one of the girls doubled over and threw up,
everybody else started gagging
and yelling.

one of the other kids
stuck his finger in the blood and tasted it.

then they all ran back to the school
to tell somebody.

I loved watching them
and knowing them better
than some of them knew themselves.
watching groups of them
growing up
getting it all figured out
then going away.
I loved so much about watching them
and loving them
and hating them.

but most of all
I loved
being the only person
who knew
what happened on the couch.

Wounded

the hole I leave
in your chest
will heal itself
without stitches
without bandages,
but not without scars.

and I'm sorry
you'll have those scars
on your otherwise
perfect body.

I'm sorry
you'll have those scars
on your otherwise
perfect little heart.

I'm sorry your eyes
will never hold somebody's dreams
the way they held mine.

but the wound I leave...
the wound I leave
will heal itself
with time.

It's the last thing I'll promise.

it will be
the only promise
I can never break.

If I End Up
Giving Up

I've tried really hard.

to keep going.

to get better.

to at least explain
what it's like
to hurt like this.

I've tried really hard
to say something
anything
to help it make sense.

but it doesn't even make sense to me.

when that darkness comes
it really does take over,
like I'm possessed
by a spirit that wants me
to give up.

it's persuasive,
it's violent
it's disgusting
and it's part of
me.

this thing
that wants me to give up...

it's part of who I am
and I'm not sure how long
I can handle knowing that
and not being able
to fix myself.

I'm afraid
I'm only going to get worse,
but I'm trying so fucking hard
to get better.

so
if I end up giving up,
I'm sorry.

in the end
sorry is the only thing
I can expect to be.

--- For Me ---

photo Sarah E. Collins

Eric Victorino is a poet, artist and musician. He was
born January 3rd, 1978 in San Jose, California.
He lives in the San Francisco Bay Area.

NAMI - National Alliance on Mental Illness
nami.org

Mental illness impacts the lives of at least one in four adults
and one in ten children. Over 60 million Americans.
NAMI works every day to save every life.

National Hopeline Network
HOPE 1-800-SUICIDE (784-2433)

National Suicide Prevention Hotline
1-800-273-TALK (273-8255)

Thank You.

Sarah Collins, Tammy Collins, Kathy Heisey, Scott Heisey, Deanna V. Rose, Mike Shea, Richard Ferry, Daniel Ponich, Connor MacFarlane, Sara Pina, Amanda Inglis and Jasen Compton, Alyx Pasquale, Johanna Olson, Luis Gomez, Mayra, Denise Miller, Kimberly Hall, Johanna Olson, Kathryn Hille, Jay Crosby, Delaney Boesch, Isaiah Hobbs, Kristin Hansen, Kyla Barkley, Kristy Sargent, Dua'a Behbehani, Belinda R. Hill, Doctor Popular, Cecilia Barbosa, Tyler Hill, Matthias Dransmann, Sergio Josue Gonzalez Jr., Ruben Tello, Judith Lynn, Sheena Marie Popowich, Christine Fran Connallon, Elaine Kimble, Jenna Rose Marie, Zuha, Devin Garabedian, Joe Giunta, Cindy Cristobal Valladares, Cynthia Marie Owen, Alison Hohman, Steve Palopoli, Molli Sullivan, Giovanni Giusti, Hannah Collins, Jack Collins, Scotty Cruse, Michael Solari, Aaron Axelsen, Jared Short, Craig Sita, Michelle Rivera, Shelby Noelle Springer, Gareth Andrew Nelson, Gary Medeiros, Vanessa J. Bahena, Dan Polvino, Mimi, Paul Hurley, David W. Smith, Nicholas Milner, Seth Chanard, Sera Jones, Matthew Charles, Nicole Henshaw, Antonio Alexander, Courtney Miles, April Maibauer, Marley, Tony Sherick, Leigh Erin Ward, Bill Brueshaber, Rachele Harmony, Michael Milne, Matthias Dransmann, Jeff Archuleta, Iwona Cyprys, Christian Dransmann, Chris Dimond, Travis Butts, Rory Isaacson, Candice Holmes, Karie Vrba, Max Martinez, Shawn Jackson, Sam Maloy, Jordan – Jo – Sedgwick, Corey De La Cruz, William Null, Courtney & Jake Martin, Chase Loren, Denise Dionisio, Keith Biro, Eric Guitard, Lauren Fant, Melissa Amejorado-Escalera, Nick Schwartzkopf, Julia Cassidy, Brandon Prest, Caitlin Vodenichar, Ryan Young, Torri Koite, Marilyn Holman, Carolyn, Alva Keogh, John Kolb, Antonia Garcia, Kaitlyn Ebert, William deBorde, Justin Martinez, Mike Drakulich, Sandra Taketa, Myriam Plante, Laurianne Audet, Marie-Noelle Audet, John Macrae, Casey Campbell, Annabelle Cummings, Davide Mielke, Lauren Fitzsimmons, Tabbitha Brown, Christen Scogin, Natalie Milton, Derrek Sutherland, Stephanie Wolfe, Matthew Thorup, Shamus Sullivan, Geneva Conway, Rebecca Grieser, Darrell Anhel, Brandon Ruth, Jocelyn Kazenko, Tara Fee, Andy Alonzo, Marie-Eve Simard, Shayna Gianas, Shanna King, Angela Natale, Deena McClusky, Jamie Lash Sherwood, Leila Farhood, Anthony Borgstahl, Marissa Vossmer, Angel Griffiths, Patrick Drakulich, Michael Schneider, Andrew Bailey, Jessica Cribb, Jessi Hodge, Carol Perkins, Ashlee Brienzo, Brad Addis, Cristina Popek, Markos Menis, Ashif Hakik, Maddy Rogers, Sabrina Cooke, Jonny Hutchings, Brianna Chapman, Chris Youngblood, Sonny Moore, Delia Marquez, TJ Tucker, Erin Noelle, Debra Shuttleworth, Cheryl M. Buchanan, Anne Ferguson, Mark Brown, Kara Douglas, Kyle Cutler, Andrea Obregon, Cebrian, Jacqueline Milom, Kellie Hiett, GiGi Leal, Mandy April Marie Gomien, Matthew Prentice, Beth Otto, Ashlea Berry, Tiffany Forsyth, Teresa Lester, Paul Vida, Lindsey Sekelsky, Greg Hansen, Saulo Osorio, Pete M. W., Klaus Dieter Golla, Martina Kosling, Noelle

Anne Shofner, Adrianna Maya, Wyatt Wood, Richey Garibay and Bryana Garibay, Nina N. Rodriguez, Howard Murphy, Matt Loney, Mike Hutchison JR, Tatum Mahoney, Ciera Shepherd, Kelsey Thompson, Roseann Codr, Jason Ybarra, Robert Volkerts, Tommy Marquez, Ron Clayton, Katelyn Booth, Jennifer Wilson-Mulz, Amber Pratt, Christyna Justice, Laticia Ruberto, Christian Stephenson, Olivia Adams, Vivian Perez, Eric Hinrichsen, Corey Crane, Cody Kniffen, Kristie Honsinger, Sierra Ann Doucett, Arthur Quinn, Erika Carson, Eugene Choi, Ashley Humphreys, Amber Lajara, Amber Barber, Richard Reed, Sean Bivins, Judy Popek, Cyndi Powell, James Mays, Tiffany Johnson, Brittany Cowell, Keith Barnard Jr., Daniela Herrera, Jake Roberson, Kevin Junga, Jennifer Rubenstein, Tony Henson, Florence Mazel, Katie Beyer, Christina Craver, Dominique Rocha, Jose Ibarra, Andrea Duran, Holly Iverson, Jon Jump, Matthew Ward, Kelli Rase, Chasity Duncan, Leslie Baker, Cindy Valladares, Mona Azliana Alimin, Steve Gleeson, Brandon Autry, Beau Clifton, Derrick Buckingham, Cherie Moya, David Smith, Kim Conley, Ashley Harrison, Zachary Jablonka, Aimee Fox, Steve Ramsdell, Kayla Karaszewski, Jessica Rosado, Mickey Blasco, Tracy Henderson, Garry Mendez, Gwen Schaller, Matt Goyra, Passenger, Sasha Garabedian, Lauren Gooch, Randall Sponsler, Becca E. Hartem, Brandon Hicks, Danyel Price, Joe Webber, Nichole Ybarra, Samantha LoCiero, Michael Barton, Elizabeth Santangelo, Mario Vigil, Kasey Weikel, Rebekah Weikel, Lavon Forrester, Ender, Kori Winchell, Tara Anello, Conal Fyfe, Joshua D. Gardner, Kate Marchand, Monica Neou, Kyle Turpin, Richard Hartley, Hyle Habdo, Audrey Kitching, John Paul Lassonde, Alberts Alksnitis, Vince Favero, Spencer Jones, Erika Joy, Amelia Aguilar, Matt Moffatt, Kyle Wyaco, Ben Winslow, Karly Chester, Shae Makinster, Amber Densmore, Shawn Jones, John Wiseman, Stephanie LoCicero, Elizabeth Amber Rodriguez, Kathy Smith, Angie-Chris Shaw-Lawson, Crystal Hoffman, Katie Fixico, Josh Neuenschwander, Cynthia Tintorri, Andrew Cruz, Cristina Orozco, Charlsey Dyer, Raleigh "Rallo" Reed, Nichola Coleman, Rebecca Smith, Jake Robertson, Kimberly Villarreal, Patrick Houtz, Matthieu Bierne, Maryam Qudus, Scott Herring, Sara Gonzales, Danielle Gillett, Jesse Smith, Brett Featherman, Angela Meza, Michele Rehmati, Joel Yelin, Sydney Fritz, Mercedes Olmo, Debbie North, Mickey Blasco, Nikole Hawkes, Megan Bos, Sam Elliott, Nuutti Nieminen, Eric Schripsema, Annah Gallegos, Valerie Giuili, Trevor Fredrickson, Kevin Judice, Tiffany Wilhelm, Lynn McDonald, Anna Larina, Holly Rogers, Tylor Fulkerson, Tracy Firth, Daniel Sternbaum, Jannet Arreguin, Noah Gabriel Horton, Grace Pearsall, Chris Barbaree, Xavier Izquierdo, Caban Sleap, Amanda Peskor, Alex Ralph, Rianne Criddle, Alex Scott, Teri McAlister, Allicia Pugh, Mike Honn, Sloan Crawford, Danielle Shryock, Samantha Suhre, Andrew Dremak, Billy Nawrocki, Sara Alleman, Guylaine Plante, Cheryl Alleman, Leigh Kiepe, Charles Strouse, Maraiah Castillo, Emily Lazar, Cory Bethune, Matt Shafer, NayNay & FooCumber, Chelsea Killea, Ben Kalember,

Cody Glover, Jon Victorino, Teddy Artinyan, Todd Cooper, Alex Pardee, Ruth Ann Cogswell, Gabriel Colbert, Kelsie Offill, Sarah Elizabeth McNeal, Andrew Seanez, Snaykbayk, Miranda Bretz & Jamez Garman, Ian Ameling, Bryna Turner, David Widener, Nigel Bradford, A Sunset Diary, Steven Lester, Ryan Mallette, Bucky Graham, Ashley Dagnone, Staff at Kaiser Permanente Adult Psych Crisis Stabilization Center Santa Clara, Dr. Matthew Wilhelm, Dr. Alex Dimitriu, Tricia Regis, Paula Tulley, Benjamin Casabianca, Jennifer Meade, Janice Greene, Gabrielle Vasquez, Valentin Aguirre, Tiffany Crupi, Patricia Barrios, Michael Lizzio, Wynter Valenty, Logan Mace, Melissa Hartman, Brian VanMatter, Jesse Hollenweger, Danielle McBrayer, Joe Pearson, Jen Casper, Bree Barnard, Natalie Lykins, Rian Borland, Brianne Waterhouse, Whitney Wilson, Alisson Boyd, Jason Carlson, Mike Howard, Courtney Sachtleben, Spinland Studios, Tori Hastings, Ronda 'Taiwo' Benjamin, James Erickson, Kara W. Roberts, Jenna Karas, Sara Miller, Travis Maahs, Travis Thompson, Amna Khan, Michael Clemenhagen, Sarah Hammer, Breanna C. Boles, Krista Farmer, Mandy Glenzer, Matthew W. Mellott, Kevin Atkinson, Suzanne Kehr, Electra Earl, Ellen Dracopoulos, Maggie Wilder, Randi Padgett, Emily Rheingans, Austen Warner, Ruben Jauregui, Brittney Martin, Ashley Muntner, TJ Sanchez, Hope Starr Selander, Connor Ragan, Shaian Mohammadi, Cory Crawford, Jennifer Ristic, Sheila Patel, David Murdock Filippini Bibee, Alicia Busse, Leah Busse, Asia Von Sonn, Claire Louise Roberts, Dant Rambo, Mathew Rocha, Bradley David Jenkins, John Minko, Corrie Bickham, Daniel Power, Kenny Powers, Logan West, Amanda Johnson, Joshua Murphy, Mathew Duey, Darin Olsen-Saouli, Abby Dubief, Tracy Parks, Stephuu Durham, Shawn Robbins, Ben Grant Ferchuk, Laura Kobayashi, Tyler Durden, Megan Ullom, Megan Kilpatrick, Tiffany Garbarini, Joshua Carter, Liza Hickey, Ksenia Semenova, Devin Tiedke, Laura Coatney, Amber Potter, Jonathon Trevino, Allicia Pugh, Yuri Beckers, Susanne Den Boer, Chris Fields, Ashley Ransome, Mitch Henderson, Lexie Smith, Patrick Paulin, Abri Avila, Chris Tulley, Caroline Lang, Paolo Kors, Sydney Bosworth, Paul Hurley, Rachael Farmer, Kira A. Madden, Giselle Noriega, Ashley Meeds, Natasha Wheelock, Jay Aguilar, Jeremy Zane Bilnoski, Jessica RaeLewis, Cassie Ferreira, Sahsha Vandetta, Shauna Pomerleau, Shannon, Danielle Wyaco, Victoria Teer, Christian Teer, Kris Coon, Kyle Brendon Sullivan, Rev. Daniel Blair-Johns, O-manda & Izzy, Alex Gonzalez, Miranda Galloway, Brenda Williamson, Megan Newsome, Stace-Ghost Atteberry, Brandon Van Auken, Tanner & Ashley Smart, Jeanine Dorn, Sonia Alvarhawk, Elizabeth Newton, Jonathon Vaca, Melissa Meeker, Daniel Bauduin, Loren Slone, Ron Laframboise, Byczkiewicz/Stradomski Family, Katy Otto, Shalise Ellis, Sara Miller, Dr. Richard F. Hassing, Aldo Notarandrea, Joshua Baldwin, Martin Lee, Julie Kalita, Josh And Tabbi Endlessly, Austin Klinker, Karen Brandt, Vikki Dyer, Dylan Park, Courtney Miles, Cat Greenham, Adriana Barron, Kathryn Wiggins, Anya Harjung, Hunter Emigh, Val,

Patrick Michael Tillman, Marchelle Seowtewa, Shawna Raye King, Jamie Pollard, Alex Jack Ralph, Gisella Cabrera, Jesse Labate, Cuphi Onguyen, Josh Cisneros, Molli Sullivan, Jerry James Stone, Patti Hynes, Kristen Spencer, Danny Rosales, Biscuit TMFS, Charlie Robbins, Kat Kilbourn, Brian Kramer, Carlos Letelier, Christy Dee, Allen Christian, Alex Walkowski, Matt Goyra, Erika Lambier, Chris Rivera, JC, Kathyrn Wiggins, Mike Bachta, Matt Galle, MTV, NAMI, Mike Marquis, Bill McGathy, Jeff Reagan, Jake Fogelnest, Stephanie Wade, Bryan Aiello, Tommie Sunshine, Art Ambush, Zerofriends, Chad Hall, Skinner, Crystal Wylde, Sara Nejatifar, Sarah Lewittin, Hipstamatic / Synthetic / Snap Magazine, K-Von, Lindsay Hazlett.

Orchard City Books & Noise
PO Box 671
Cambell, CA
95009-0671

Trading Sunshine For Shadows

Also By Eric Victorino

&

Coma Therapy

&

Trading Shadows For Sunshine

Available in eBook and iBook formats
as well as spoken word recording
in the iTunes music store and Amazon.com

Audio CD available from OrchardCity.net